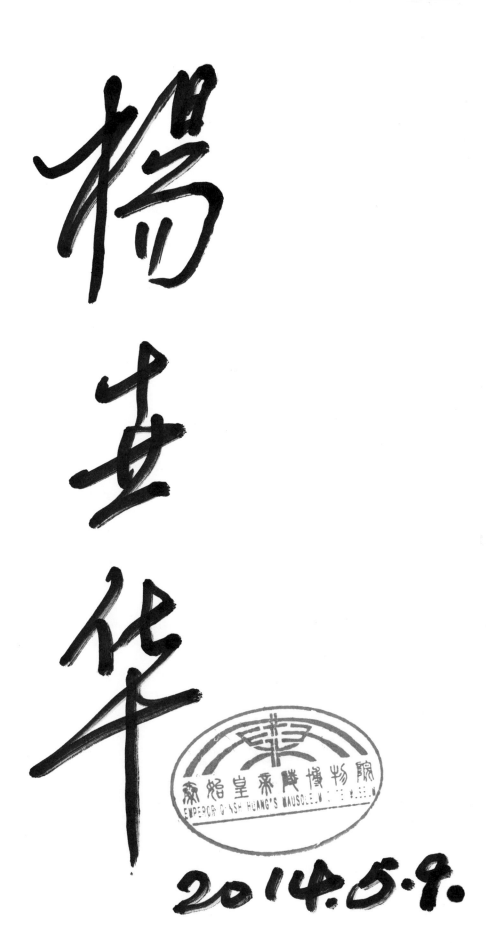

楊甚華

秦始皇兵馬俑博物館
EMPEROR QINSH HUANG'S MAUSOLEUM SITE MUSEUM

2014.5.9.

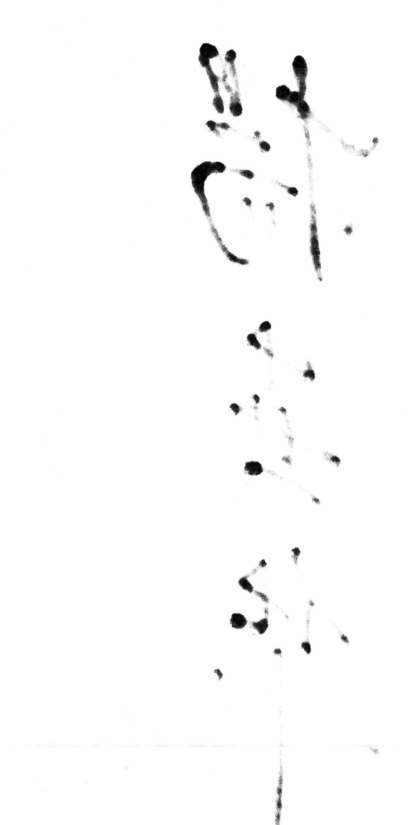

TREASURES
OF THE MAUSOLEUM
OF THE FIRST
QIN EMPEROR

EMPEROR QIN SHI HUANG'S
MAUSOLEUM SITE
MUSEUM

SHAANXI PUBLISHING MEDIA GROUP
SHAANXI TRAVEL & TOURISM PRESS

FOREWORD

A Journey to Discover the Treasures of the Great Qin Empire

Since Emperor Qin Shi Huang reunited the once divided country, all the best treasures then have been gathered up to his empire which however lasted only 15 years. The first emperor of the short-lived empire rested in his underground palace eternally, with the company of innumerable treasures. Thousands of years have passed since those treasures were brought to light again. Indeed, not every one is lucky enough to witness the archeological discovery made on site. As for the treasures, people often feel regret, if not sentimental, for not meeting them earlier or never seeing them at all in their entire life. It is this feeling that drives us to present this book to you.

The treasures of Qin Empire are as valuable as thousands of years' time behind them. The book offers a general guide for you to discover all the amazing treasures. No matter they are vivid terracotta figures, the weapons as sharp as ever or the impressive and delicate gold *danglu* (gold decoration on horse face), the visual information delivers the rich and profound history of the Great Qin Empire in a vibrant, refined and long-lasting way, leading you into the past as if it was 209B.C. in ancient China.

It is not an exaggeration to compare the book, *Treasures of the Mausoleum of the First Qin Emperor* to a movable treasure house of the Great Qin Empire. It is a perfect documental souvenir to keep after your visit of Emperor Qin Shi Huang's Mausoleum Site Museum and will also enrich your collection of books as a rare shining cultural gem.

The book is the epitome of 3000-year civilization of ancient China, especially the Qin dynasty. With the joint efforts made by both world-class masters of photography and the photographers working on the archeological sites of Terracotta Warriors for half a century, it collects all the breath-taking moments of discovery captured through the lens, making a visual feast with refined details beyond human's eyesight.

The book serves as a new milestone among other culture-themed books published by Emperor Qin Shi Huang's Mausoleum Site Museum. Driven by the concept of *"cultural post"* promoted by our museum, it is specially and exquisitely designed for a general readership in the form of a combination of both illustrations and words. Foreign friends who have been given the book as a present speak highly of it as it tells the legend of the terracotta army.

A set of *zhaoshentie* (ID card used in Qin dynasty) of the Great Qin Empire is attached inside as a gift. For the first time, *zhaoshentie* reveals to visitors a history of nowadays household registration system in China, highlighting the great contributions made by Emperor Qin Shi Huang as the first emperor in Chinese history.

Different from other similar tourist souvenirs, *zhaoshentie* is printed in the bird-worm seal script and each with a serial number, laden with rich cultural connotations. We believe it will definitely leave you deep impression even years from today.

After 400 days of efforts on preparation and editing, the book *Treasures of the Mausoleum of the First Qin Emperor* is now published with an initial circulation of 10,000 books, which seems to be rather a small number compared with 6 millions visitors of the mausoleum each year. It is time to bring this souvenir home and keep a long-lasting memory.

CONTENTS

Back then,

Shang Yang (the statesman of the state of Qin) initiated a reform in state Qin,

Since then *zhaoshentie* came into being.

Issued by the government,

It was a smooth and polished bamboo board

Inscripted with details like head portrait and origins, etc.

Anyone who wanted to enter state Qin,

Must hold his own board,

Otherwise he would be refused to enter.

编 04369 号

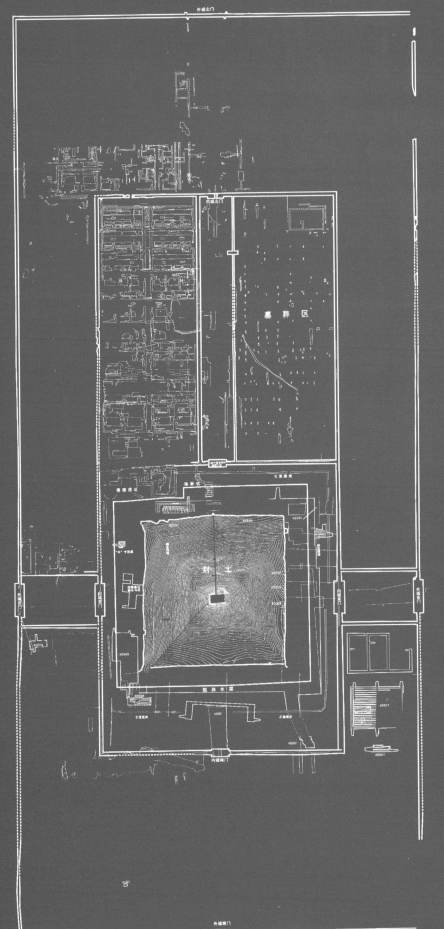

The
Mausoleum of
Emperor
Qin Shi Huang

The Map Indicating the Geological Relation between the Mount Li and the Mausoleum of Emperor Qin Shi Huang

As a branch of northern Qinling Mountains, Mount *Li* is a result from the orogeny of the Himalayas. It is 25*km* across from east to west, seven kilometers from north to south, with an elevation of around 1,000*m* above the sea level. The rugged topography leads to the alternation of hills and trenches, producing south-north valleys which nurture rivers and streams. The tomb of Emperor Qin Shi Huang sits on the pluvial fans scoured by the rivers.

Ying Zheng (259-210B.C.), Emperor Qin Shi Huang, came to the throne at the age of 13 and began to hold the power when he was 21. With enormous military power and financial strength, Ying Zheng spent 10 years to finally defeat and merge six states including Han, Zhao, Wei, Chu, Yan and Qi one after another, completing the great cause of reunification. The first unitary multi-ethnic dynasty governed by centralized feudal monarch in Chinese history was established since then. He died of illness in July, 210B.C. in Shaqiu Pingtai (the great Pingtai area in today's Hebei province) and was buried in September of the same year at the north of Mount Li, five kilometers east of Lintong district in Xi'an, Shaanxi province.

According to the biographic sketch of Emperor Qin Shi Huang in *Records of the Historian*, that "as soon as the First Emperor became king of Qin, excavations and building had been started at Mount Li, while after won the empire more than 700,000 conscripts from all parts of the country worked there. They dug through three subterranean streams and poured molten copper for the outer coffin, and the tomb was filled with models of palaces, pavilions and offices, as well as fine vessels, precious stones and rarities. Artisans were ordered to fix up crossbows so that any thief breaking in would be shot. All the country's streams, the Yellow River and the Yangtze were reproduced in quicksilver and by some mechanical means made to flow into a miniature ocean. The heavenly constellations were shown above and the regions of the earth below. The candles were made of whale oil to ensure their burning for the longest possible time"[1] , it is evident that he began to build his mausoleum from the very beginning of his rulership (246B.C.).

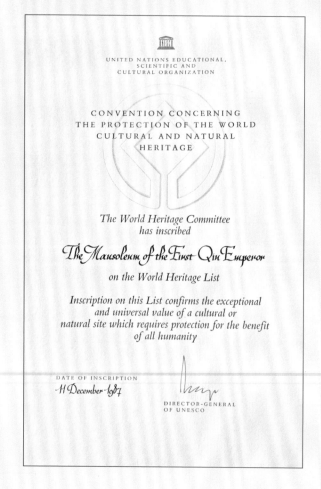

| Certificate of World Heritage

Covering 56.25km^2, it took 37 years and around 700,000 labors to build Emperor Qin Shi Huang's mausoleum, standing as the grandest with the richest burial objects among all the imperial tombs throughout Chinese history. It mainly consists of subterranean palace, sealing soil, city walls and gates, various burial objects, burial pits, all kinds of affiliated architectures and mausoleum feods. The whole mausoleum was well designed and rich in burial objects. The layout of tomb and arrangement for the ritual facilities, both traditional and innovative, has a far-reaching impact on the imperial mausoleums of subsequent dynasties. At present, there are already 149 burial pits, 196 burial tombs have been discovered, including the Bronze Chariots pit, the Rare Birds and Beasts pits, the Barns pits in small and large scales, the Stone Armor pit, the Warriors and Horses pits and other sacrificial pits. All those together build a massive treasure house. On March 4th 1961, the State Council declared Emperor Qin Shi Huang's mausoleum a major historical and culture sites protected at the national level, one of the first sites in the country. The mausoleum including the pits of terracotta army was listed as one of the UNESCO World Cultural Heritage sites on December 7th 1987.

[1] From Yang Xianyi and Gladys Yang's translation of Selections from Records of the Historian

Portrait of Emperor Qin Shi Huang

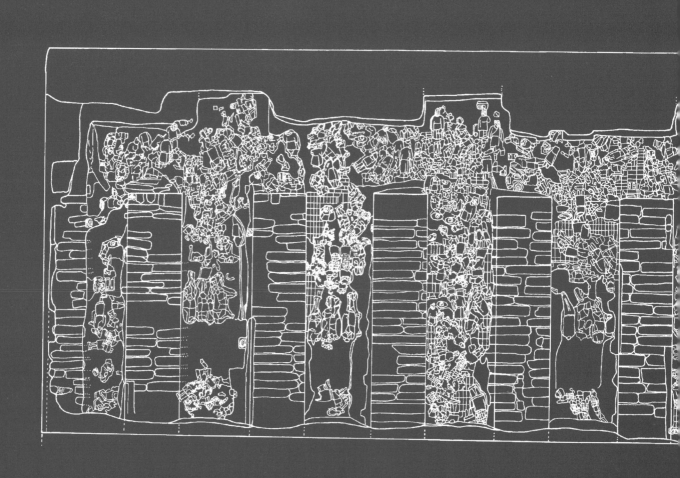

Warriors and Horses Burial Pits

Warriors and horses burial pits, $1.5km$ east of Qin tomb, are the earliest discoveries in the mausoleum. The three pits were labeled as Pit No.1, No.2 and No.3 respectively in order of discovery dates. Covering a total area of $20,000km^2$, the pits contain 8,000 life-size terracotta figures and horses. It is the enormous scale of the tomb and its exquisite sculptures that continue to captivate visitors greatly and make it renowned as the *Eighth Wonder of the World* and a great archeological discovery of the 20th century.

A huge number of chariots and terracotta figures were buried in these pits. According to previous excavations and trial excavation, there are 140 chariots, 560 chariot horses, 116 cavalry horses and 7,000 various warrior figures. All these remains provide precious and rich sources for us to deepen our understanding of the development in troops, weaponry and societies from late Warring State period to the Qin dynasty.

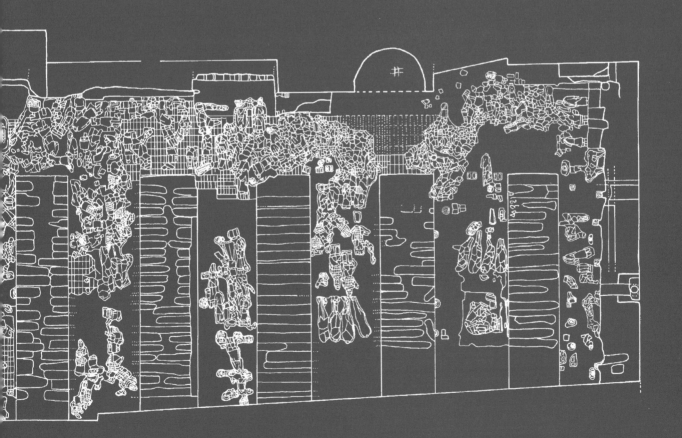

Panorama of Pit No.1

A local farmer in Xiyang village of Lintong district in Xi'an accidently discovered Pit No.1 when he drilled for water in March 1974. Later, after further scientific exploration and trial excavation, it was confirmed as a pit measuring $230m$ long and $62m$ wide, covering an area of $14,260m^2$. According to the arrangement of terracotta warriors and horses unearthed in trial excavation, the pit was estimated to house around 6,000 figures as well a great quantity of bronze weaponry.

Panorama of Pit No.2

Part of Pit No.2

Located 20m north to the eastern end of pit No.1, Pit No.2 was discovered in April 1976. This L-shaped pit measures 124m east to west and 98m south to north with an area of some 6,000km². It is estimated that the terracotta warriors and horses in this pit amount to 1,300 figures. The great variety makes it top notch among all the three.

Panorama of Pit No.3

Pit No.3 was discovered in May 1976, 25*m* north to the western end of Pit No.1. In the shape of a Chinese character 凹 (concave shape), it is of smaller scale with an area of 520*km²*, containing 72 terracotta warriors and horses. Some scholars believe that it served as a headquarter for the army, known as *junmu* (military commanding office) in ancient China, directing the warriors in Pit No.1 and No.2. While others think it was used as a *junshe* (military shrine) for sacrifice before the army went on an expedition.

Part of Pit No.3

Terracotta Figures of High-ranking Officers

High-ranking officers are also known as Figures of Generals. There were 10 unearthed in total, nine in Pit No.1 and one in No.2, among which two are dressed in battle robes and seven wear armors. Some of them hold long swords with their hands crossed before their bellies, while some have their arms in a natural position and hold swords with the right hands. These generals all wear double-layered robes under colorful fish-scaled armors, and high caps decorated with pheasant's tail feathers (*heguan* cap), indicating their highest status in the army.

Heguan(A Cap Decorated with Pheasant's Tail Feather)

Terracotta Figures of Middle-ranking Officers

Terracotta Figures of Middle-ranking Officers wear double-slab cap and are dressed in armors. Some of them stand next to the high-ranking officers as their deputies. Others, having strong body and uplifted spirit, stand along with soldiers like directors.

Terracotta Figures of Low-ranking Officers

All wearing single-slab caps, low-ranking officers are in two types: light infantrymen wearing no armors and heavy infantrymen in armors without colorful patterns. They each holds a sword in one hand and a long weapon like spear or *ge* (dagger-axes) in the other.

Terracotta Figures in Battle Robe

The total number of unearthed warriors in battle robe is 433, with 397 in Pit No.1 and 36 in Pit No.2. This kind of warriors is also known as light infantrymen without armors and helmets. They are fashioned with high conical hair bun on the right side of the head, carrying arrow quiver on the back, holding crossbow or long weapon in hand. With the advantage of swiftness and flexibility, they usually serve as vanguard in troops to carry out raids.

Terracotta Figures of Standing Archers

Standing archers are standing infantrymen in shooting position. Currently, only one was unearthed in Pit No.1 and 172 in the east of Pit No.2, all with a height around 180cm. The standing archers, with hair bun and in light battle robe, posture as if they were about to shoot, which is in perfect accordance with historical records.

Kneeling archers are kneeling infantrymen holding crossbow. Altogether 160 were unearthed, most of which are arranged in rows at the eastern end of Pit No.2. In the heart of the military matrix, they form a crossbowmen matrix together with standing archers. Compared with standing archers, kneeling archers on the right knew are easier to aim targets and less likely to be spotted by enemies, making their posture perfect for defense or ambush. All these kneeling figures are vivid reflections of infantrymen training in ancient China.

Terracotta Figures of Kneeling Archers Incised with Chinese Character Zhao (朝)

Terracotta Figure of Green-faced Kneeling Archer

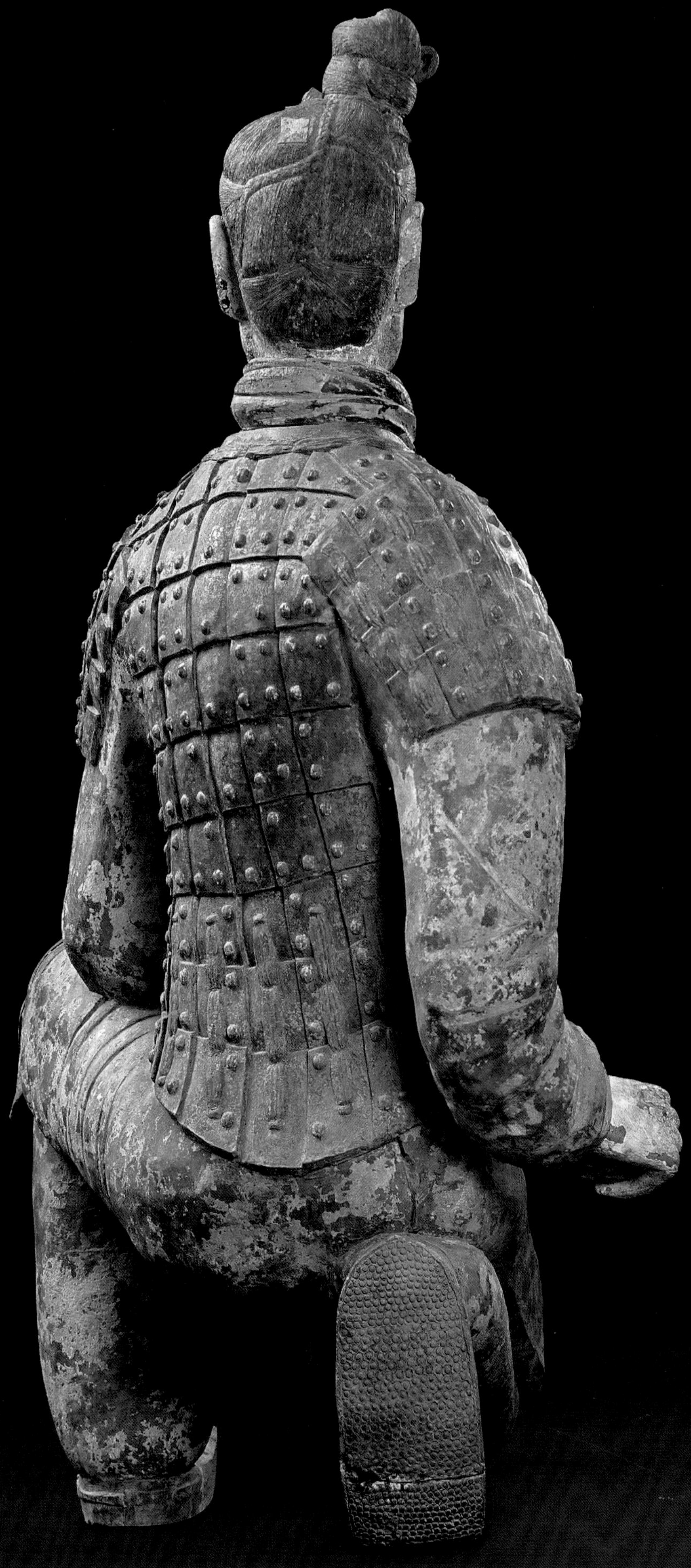

Terracotta Figures of Armored Warriors

Armored warriors are also known as figures of heavy infantrymen. They have been unearthed in the number of 1,300, falling into three types: warriors with conical hair bun, warriors with flat hair bun on one side, and warriors with *jieze* turbans. Heavy infantrymen are the main force in an army; and their weapons vary according to their positions and ranks in a troop. Some of them hold crossbow and others hold long weapons including bows, *ge* (dagger-axes), spears, halberds, *pi* (a double-bladed spear with a long shaft) or *shu* (a metal-headed club with a tapering tail).

Terracotta Figures of Armored Warriors

Terracotta Figures of Cavalrymen and Saddled Cavalry Horses

Those cavalrymen and saddled horses were unearthed in Pit No.2. The costume of the cavalrymen is the earliest archeological record to date on *hufu* (*hu* refers to the northern minorities living in the northwestern part of ancient China; *fu* means costume). The unearthed bronze arrowheads, crossbows and fragmental bronze swords show that Qin cavalrymen were mainly equipped with crossbows and short swords. The unearthed terracotta horses are low in height; however with heavy heads, muscular body and well developed legs, they are in great shape for both speedy driving and riding. Qin dynasty had a strict rule that the height of saddled horse should be no less than 130*cm*. Most of them were selected and trained in governmental barns.

Back to the Spring and Autumn period, Qin was renowned for its powerful military strength, wielding thousands of chariots, hundreds of thousands of horses and millions of infantrymen. Relying on the mighty troop, Emperor Qin Shi Huang accomplished the great cause of reunification by defeating the other six states. Large number of chariots buried in Terracotta Army pits, 50 in Pit No.1, 89 in Pit No. 2 and one in Pit No. 3, are the best evidence of Qin's glorious past. All of the chariots unearthed are wood, single-shafted, double-wheeled and led by four horses in front. A chariot consists of three parts, the weight-bearing part, the movement-facilitating part, namely wheels and axles, and the horse harness.

Chariot Remains

Being categorized into four types, the chariots unearthed share the same basic construction, but differ in charioteers and decorations. Like the ordinary chariots, the command chariots are also pulled by a team of four horses and in light weight designed for attack. But they are luxurily decorated with refined colorful patterns and hanging bells and drums. Each chariot is equipped with an officer, a charioteer and a warrior on the right.

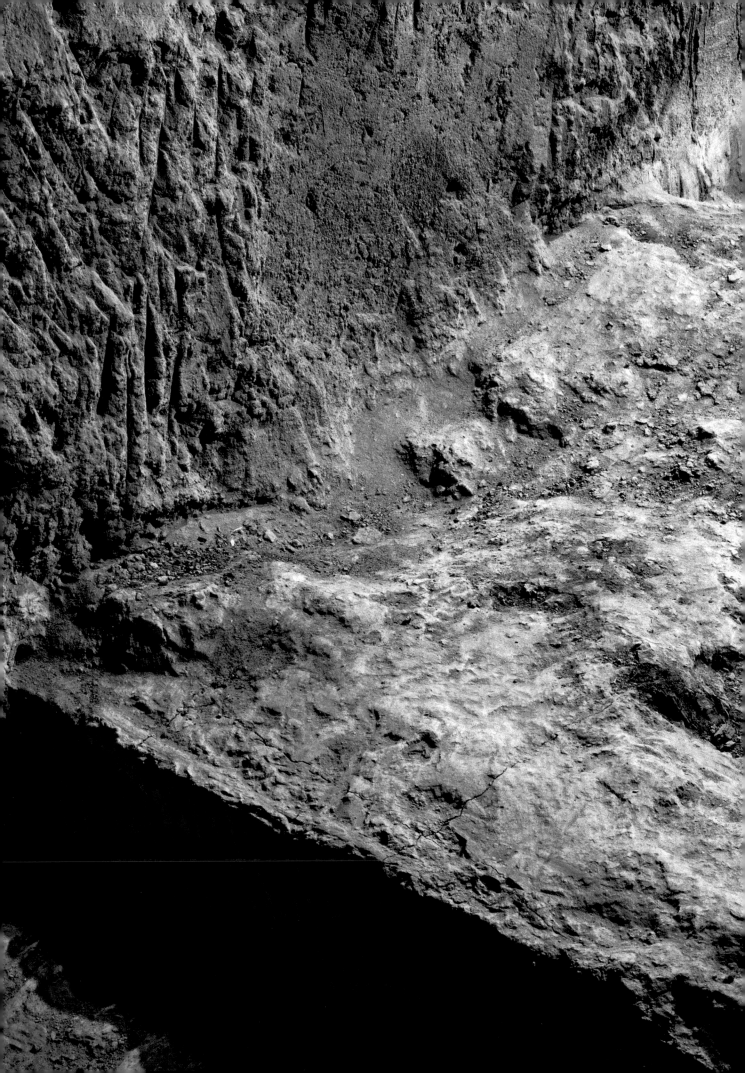

Chariot Remains

The chariot remains excavated feature wheels with short axles. Without a canopy and cloth, the chariot is pulled by a team of four horses, running at a high speed. Each is equipped with one charioteer, one warrior on the left and one on the right, lining up in a row.

Chariot Remains

The chariots unearthed in Pit No. 3 are equipped with four terracotta figures lining up in two rows, one charioteer in the front row and one officer in the center of the back row with one warrior on each side. The officer wears a double-slab long cap and a chest armor painted with colorful lace. The rest all wear armors and single-slab long caps. The high rank of this chariot is suggested by its painted pattern and canopy.

A Left Warrior on Chariot

A Right Warrior on Chariot

Each chariot is equipped with a charioteer, a warrior on the left and a warrior on the right lining up horizontally. All of them are in standing position with the warriors holding crossbow, spears or *ge* (dagger-axes).

Terracotta Figures of Charioteers

Every single one of the hundred or so wooden chariots is equipped with a charioteer responsible for driving the chariot to ensure its safety and flexible movement. It is arguably said that driver's technique is directly related with the result of a war. So the charioteers back then were strictly selected and trained to make sure all the chariots were under perfect control.

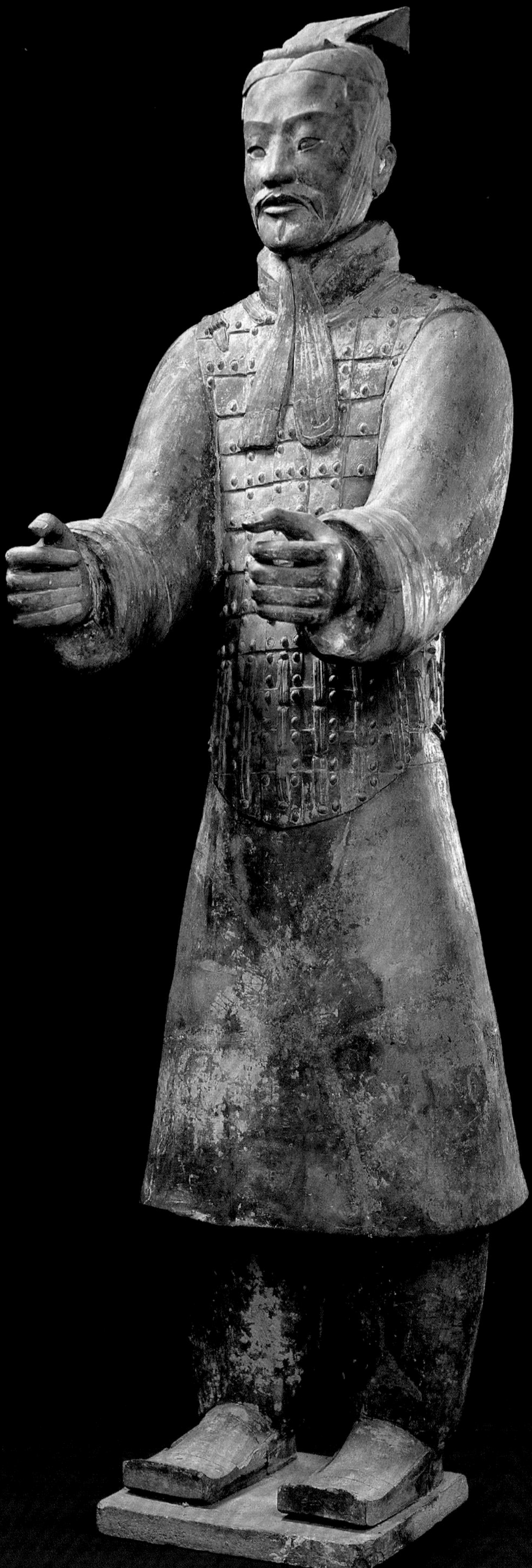

Chariot Horses

Each chariot is pulled by a team of four horses measuring 210*cm* long and 172*cm* high. They are in the same size as the horses unearthed in the Stable pit at the eastern end of the mausoleum, indicating that the chariot horses were molded after real ones. In small size, they have short neck and wide head, known as *hequ* Horse living around the Tao River in today's Gansu province.

The striking feature of terracotta warriors is its realistic depicting of both body and spirit. Unlike the identical mass-produced faces in group figure sculpturing, the terracotta artisans made a breakthrough and presented various distinct characters by analyzing individual facial features and characteristics of people with different identities. The analysis of facial features of terracotta warriors shows that Qin people's faces were in eight basic shapes, resembling eight Chinese characters *mu* (目), *guo* (国), *yong* (用), *jia* (甲), *tian* (田), *you* (由), *shen* (申) and *feng* (风) which also reflect the general facial features shared by Chinese people at that time.

Guo-shaped (国) face is rectangular, featuring wide forehead, broad cheek, high cheekbone and firm chin. There is usually handlebar moustache between nose and upper lip and the rough five sense organs make the person looks very honesty and reliable. It is a face shape commonly seen in rural areas of Shaanxi province where the villagers have wide forehead and cheekbone, plump facial muscle, dark eyebrows, big eyes, short nose bridge and big nose tip, thick lip and reddish facial skin, suggesting health, strength and honesty.

Yong-shaped (用) face is quite similar with the *guo*-shaped featuring rectangular face, but with a flatter cheek and chin. This kind of warriors feature flat and long face, broad forehead, thin chin, long and thin eyes and big mouth with thin lips. Some of them have a longer rectangular frowning face with a flat and wide chin tilting up. They keep their eyes wide open staring at the front vigilantly and sharply. Others feature plump cheek, thin eyebrows above small eyes, and little mouth with thin lips. The delicate five-sense organs don't quite match with the chubby face but look very cute.

Tian-shaped (田) face is a round square face. Some warriors of this type have plump cheek with solemn and dignified expression; the others have wider face with raised forehead, tip of the nose, chin and cheekbone and sunken eyes and mouth, revealing the obvious curves of muscles and bones. Usually, the warriors with this type of face are small in size yet very strong.

Mu-shaped (目) face is also commonly seen among all the terracotta warriors, just following the previous three types in number. Long and narrow, this type of face has delicate five-sense organs. Some of the faces are long with thin eyebrows and eyes, thin lips with handlebar moustache and a little stubble on the chin. The warriors with this type of face have round hair bun, standing with dignity in a natural way. Compared with strong warriors with big head and wide face, they represent delicate beauty instead of boldness. Some warriors have long yet chubby face with thin eyebrow and big eyes as well as plump lips as if they were fresh soldier while some have high cheekbone, thin face with wrinkles crawling on the forehead and handlebar moustache above the upper lip and three spot-like beards on the chin, suggesting that they are experienced veterans.

Jia-shaped (甲) faces accounts for a large proportion. It is like a trapezoid with wide cheekbone and both ends of the face are relatively narrow, a handsome face liked by many.

Shen-shaped (申) faces are few in number, featuring full forehead, plump cheek, high cheekbone, thin and long chin, handlebar moustache, big eyes with curvy eyebrow and genuine smile, delivering vividness to the viewers.

You-shaped (由) face is in small proportion. It is characterized by long face, narrow forehead, thin cheek and chubby chin. The high cheekbone, small chin, tilted mustache, big eyes and smiling face present a very vivid personality.

*One Thousand Figures
with One Thousand
Distinct Faces*

One Thousand Figures with One Thousand Distinct Faces

Qin terracotta warriors have vivid and vigorous facial features, resulting in "one thousand figures with one thousand distinct faces". It not only reveals individual characteristics but also reflects artisans' acute observation of life. Warriors' distinct facial features represent geographic differences: for example, those having wild forehead, thick lips, broad cheek and single eyelid were mostly from Qin on the central Shaanxi plain; while those with round chin, thin lips, vigilant expression were originated from *bashu* (today's Sichuan province). Double eyelids are rare among Qin terracotta warriors, who have thick single eyelids. This is also in accordance with the fact that the main fighting force of Qin army consists of people from central Shaanxi plain.

ne Thousand Figures
th One Thousand
stinct Faces

Qin people cherished their moustache very much. Back then almost all of the ordinary male adults grew a beard, except criminals who were forced to shave off. The beards of Qin warriors can be categorized into whisker, moustache, long beard and handlebar moustache. All the different types of moustache of terracotta warriors were inspired by but artistically exaggerated from the observation of real life. As opposed to realistic western sculptures, the moustaches of terracotta warriors are in an impressionistic manner, reflecting the unique aesthetic value and interests of Qin people.

Ancient Chinese valued their hairstyles for they viewed one's hairstyle as a symbol of status and there was no exception for Qin people. The terracotta warriors in battle robe and some armored terracotta warriors wear buns on the top right side of their heads, which are known as conical hair buns by shape, though there is no exact record about its name in previous literature. The fact that the bun is on the top right side is likely to be related to the tradition of Qin people that the right is favored. Another flat hair bun style is shared by officers, charioteers, cavalrymen and some of the armored warriors. However a high-ranking officer is distinguished by his unique flat hair bun, which is made by gathering all the hair up to the back of head, folding and coiling them into a hair-cone which is fixed in the headdress with a hair clasp. The little cubes on the hair bun look like hairpins made of bones. The varieties of terracotta warrior's hairstyles suggest the great importance Qin people had attached to their hair.

Hairstyles of Warriors

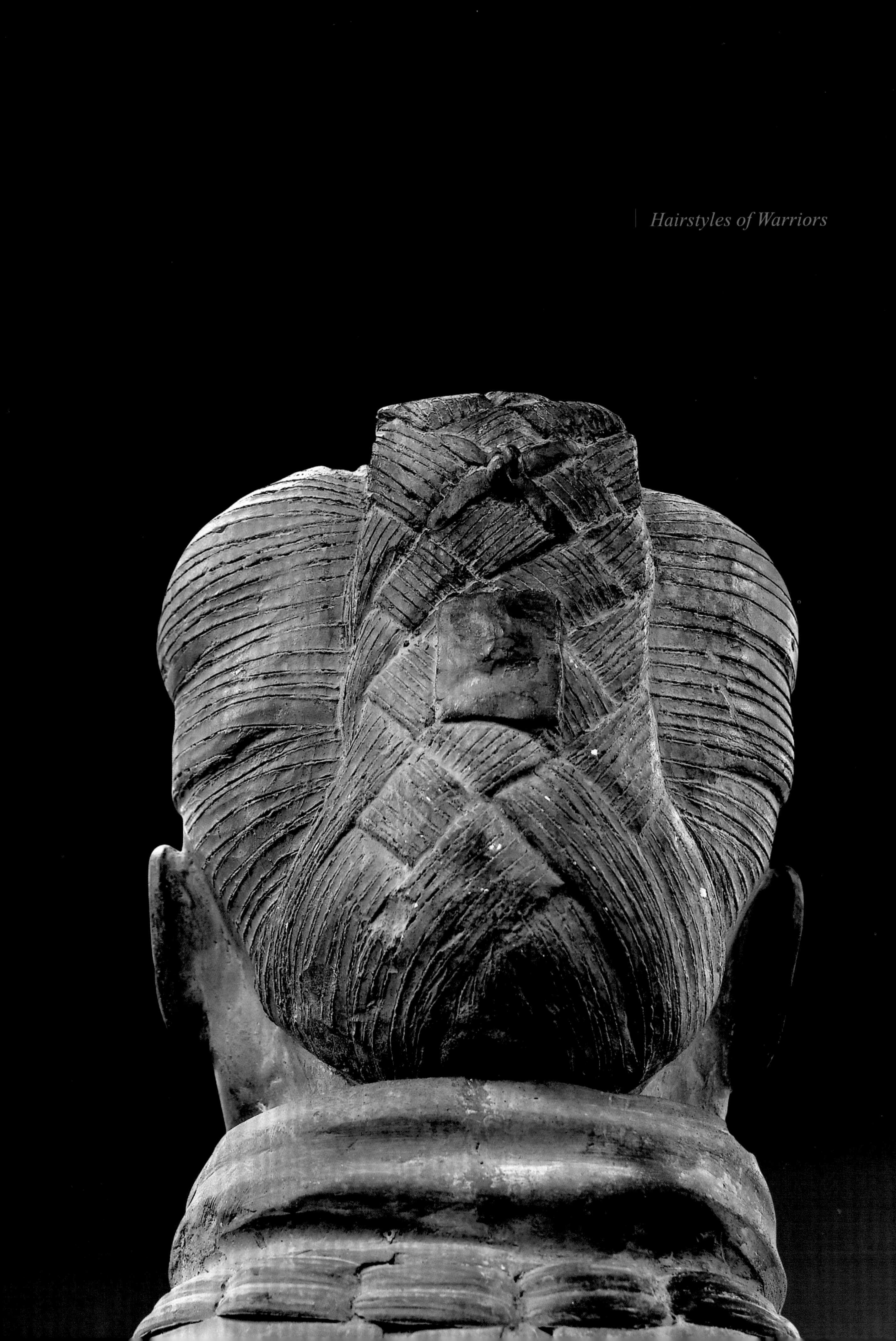

Many of the terracotta warriors were equipped with armors. Six groups of armors have been identified corresponding to rank and military division, including the armors for high-ranking officers, middle-ranking officers, low-ranking officers, chariot warriors, infantrymen and cavalrymen. The fact that life-size terracotta warriors wear armors in the same size of the real ones provides us with precious data to study the protection equipment of Qin army.

In terracotta warriors' pits, few armors for high-ranking and middle-ranking officers have been found and they are made by weaving plates on top of armors for better protection. Other types of armors, all formed by plates directly, have been discovered in large number, which were assumed to be the mainstay in Qin army at that time.

Iron armors were used by many states since the Warring States period except by Qin. According to archeological data, although large amount of iron production tools have been unearthed, iron weaponry were rarely seen and no iron armor has been excavated yet. Back then the six states in Shandong began to manufacture iron weaponry and helmets; however, Qin mainly used iron in production tools. Therefore, it is speculated that the Qin armors were made of leather.

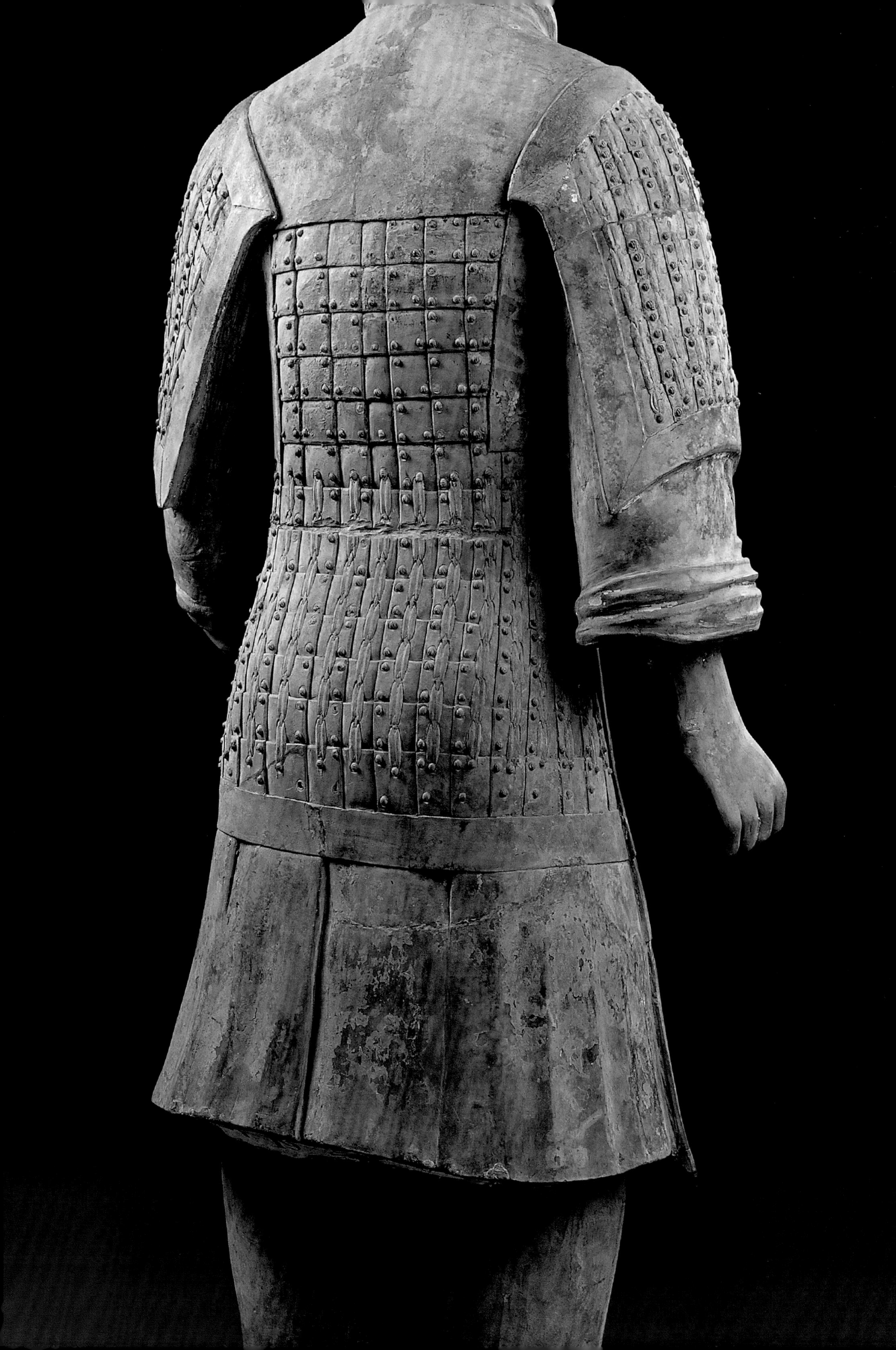

Armors for High-ranking Officers

Eight out of ten high-ranking officers excavated from Pit No.1 and No.2 wear armors, and all of them are made of leather. The armors are lined with exquisite geometrical pattern and can be divided into two types, having pauldrons over the shoulders and ones without pauldrons.

Armors with pauldrons over the shoulders are made up of the front and the back pieces. The front piece has a triangular extension decorated with colorful motif on all sides. The right shoulder and the chest are connected by a button knot attached with a ribbon knot. There are in total eight ribbon knots scattered on the chest, the shoulder and the back. This type of armor is rich in color and is delicately made with small plates. Armor without pauldron has only a front piece fastened by straps. The armor is made from a whole piece of leather, attached with plates in square, rectangular and trapezoid shapes in the center, leaving an edge of 6*cm* wide. It consists of black plates and red straps with exquisite geometric patterns.

Armors for Middle-ranking Officers

They are divided into two types. The first type is chest armor with straps, composed of chest, back and shoulder parts. The chest and back parts are made of whole piece of leather. The shoulder part and the border of the armor are lined with geometric patterns. It consists of black brown plates and vermillion straps. Most of the plates are in square or rectangular shape while a few are in irregular such as fish-scale shape; therefore, the armor is also named as colorful fish scale armor. The other type is colorful fish-scale armors with the front and back piece in the same length.

Armors for Low-ranking Officers

This type of armors is made by weaving large plates together, and there is no colorful motif in any edge. It is composed of the front chest, the back and shoulder pieces without border decoration and cloth cover. One set of armor consists of 195 ~ 229 plates in square, rectangular and irregular shapes.

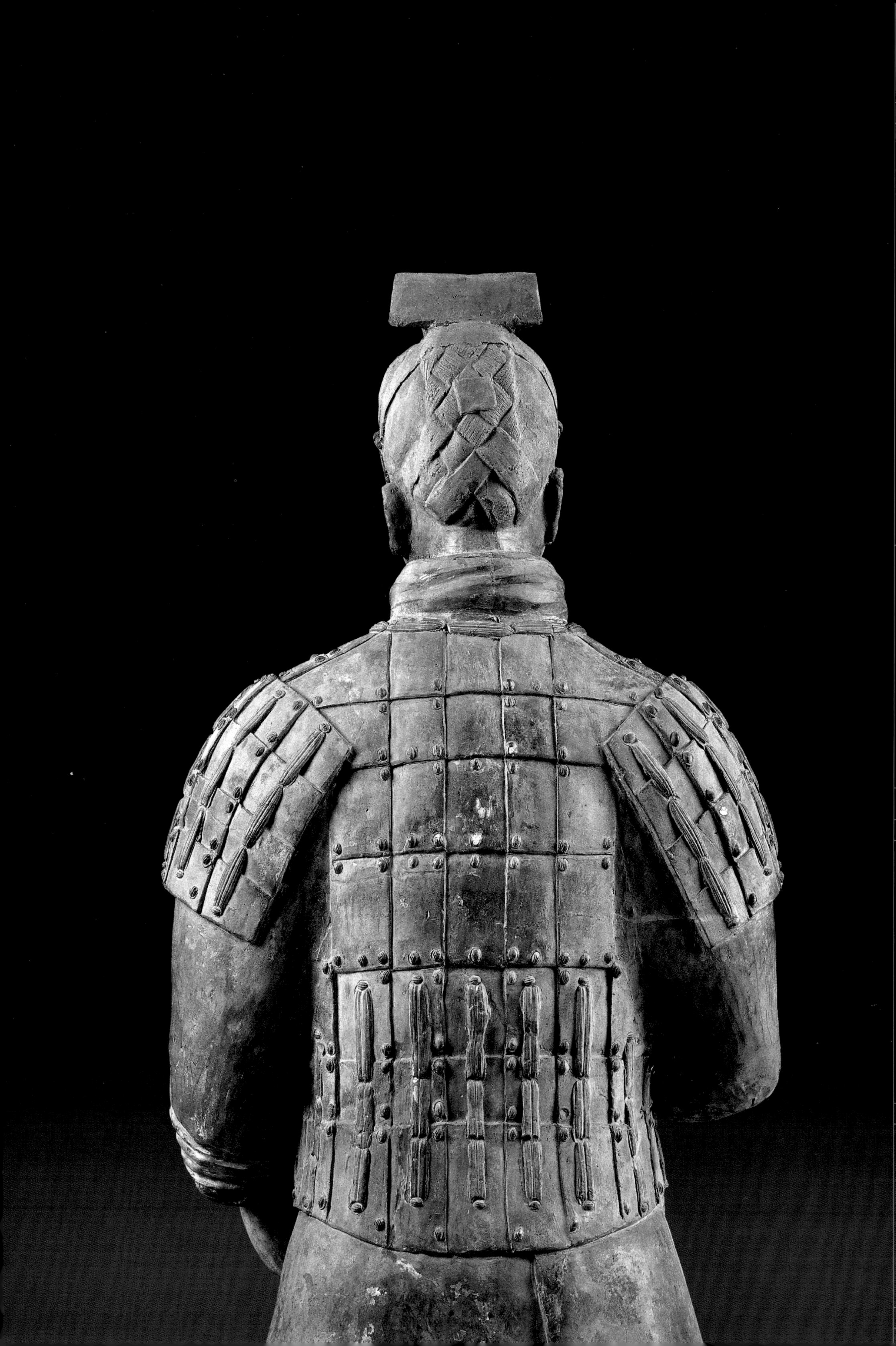

Charioteers wear two kinds of armors: one with and one without pauldrons. An armor without pauldrons consisting of the front and the back pieces is made up of 197 plates in total. The one with pauldrons covers five body parts: the front, the back, the arms and wrists, and the hand and collar. The plates for pauldrons are movable, allowing the movements of waist and arms. This type of armor is made up of 327 plates.

An Armor with Pauldrons
on a Charioteer

An Armor without Pauldrons
on a Charioteer

The broken terracotta warriors and horses pieces present difficulties in repairing but also provide opportunity for us to study closely the manufacture of the terracotta figures.

Three steps have been taken to make terracotta figures. First, mold clay into a rough figure; second, patch with more clay and work on the details after the second molding; third, assemble separately-manufactured head, hands and torso together to complete a figure. After the figures are dried in the shade, they are roasted in kilns at a temperature of 1,000℃, and then painted.

As for the terracotta figures as a whole, they were molded and sculptured by hand. The figures were roasted in kilns near the pits because the clay seems to be local and is mixed with silica sand. However, to date no kiln to roast the figures has been found yet.

Judging from the crack on the heads of the terracotta warriors, heads were made through joint sealing technique.

Connect Terracotta Figure's Head with Its Body

Judging from the connecting method between a head and its torso, we assume that heads were manufactured separately. After the original molding, ear, hair bun, plait, hat were attached and the details of a face were sculptured later. The five-sense organs were finely carved and decorated on top of the preliminary mold to present distinct personalities and emotions of the figures. Although heads were made from mold, after detailed sculpturing, no two faces look alike. Therefore, the terracotta warriors are famous for their one thousand distinct faces.

fashioned by coiling technique. Head and arms were then added to the torso to form a whole figure.

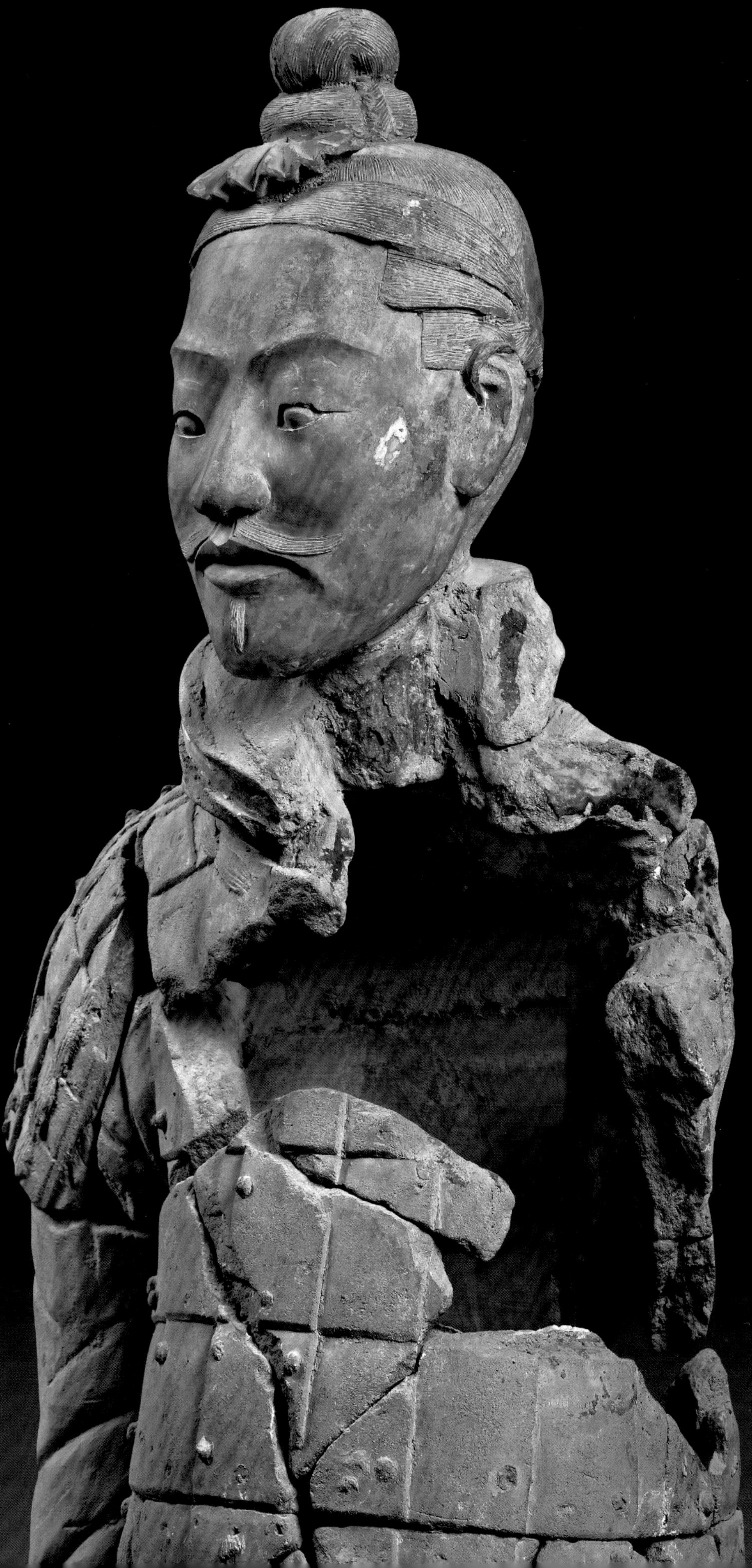

Terracotta figures were originally painted in bright colors. Now only traces of pigments can be seen on some figures. According to a rough analysis, many colors have been employed in warriors' costume, including green, vermilion, purplish red, pink, pink lilac, sky blue, white and chocolate for the upper body. The lapel, sleeve and collar of a costume are lined with colorful patterns. The trousers are usually in green, red, sky blue, purplish red and white, etc. The costume of terracotta figures were rich in various colors, among which pink, vermillion, purplish red and sky blue are the most frequently used and form the main pigments of terracotta figures' costume.

No evident difference of color was found between costume of officers and ordinary warriors, neither between different types of troops. Hence, it can be said that there was no particular requirement for the colors of different types of warriors.

We cannot confirm the material of Qin costume just by studying the terracotta warriors' costume. Although the relevant literature indicates that the civilians and soldiers' costume were made of silk, it is believed that most of the poor people were still dressed in inexpensive hand-woven clothes made from linen fabrics. Both documents and artifacts prove no strict hierarchy formulated in terms of the color and material of clothes because the Qin dynasty was in a time when the old social system was toppled and new feudal costume hierarchy had not been established. This was no longer the case in the early years of the West Han dynasty. It was the lack of costume hierarchy that allowed its diversity in color and material.

Painted Terracotta Figures

Painted Terracotta Figures

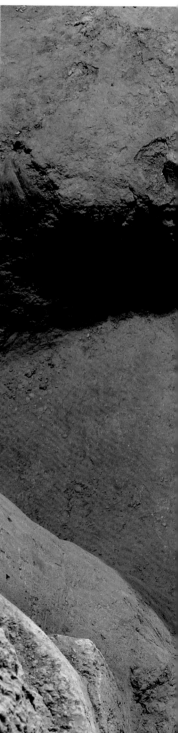

Painted Terracotta Figures

Nearly 40,000 bronze weapons were unearthed from the pits, most of which are arrowheads along with swords, *ge* (dagger-axes), spears, *ji* (Halberd), *pi* (double-bladed spear with a long shaft), *shu* (club), *yue* (battle axe), and crossbows in good quality. They can be categorized into three types by function: short-distance weapons, long-handled weapons and long-range shooting weapons.

Bronze Sword

Bronze sword is used for short-distance fighting. To date, 22 of them have been unearthed. This sword was excavated from Pit No.1, measuring 90.8cm long. The body of a sword is narrow and long, with stronger piercing ability compared with that of previous dynasties. Qin swords contain high percentage of tin, making their surfaces in bluish white. The chromium oxide coating preserves a sword's original sharpness after being buried underground for more than 2,000 years. This technique was employed in China some 2,000 years earlier than that in Europe.

Gold Hook

This weapon 71.2*cm* in length was unearthed from east of Pit No.1. The blades on both sides make it flexible and useful to kill by both pushing and pulling. However, compared with sword, it is more suitable for short-distance fight and defense. The weapon is in a shape of a hook as described in ancient literature. As gold hooks were invented in Wu state in the Spring and Autumn period, they are also termed as Wu hooks.

Spear (II)

This is a bronze spear unearthed from Pit No.3, measuring 17.5*cm* long. Spear is an extremely powerful weapon. Five bronze spears and one iron spear have been unearthed from Pit No.1, all of which are in standardized specification with sharp blades and smooth surface in silver white.

Ge (Dagger-axes)

Ge is a long-shaft dagger-axe which can be used to kill enemy by pulling. This one was excavated from Pit No.1, measuring 26.7 *cm* long incised with Chinese characters in small seal script calligraphic style.

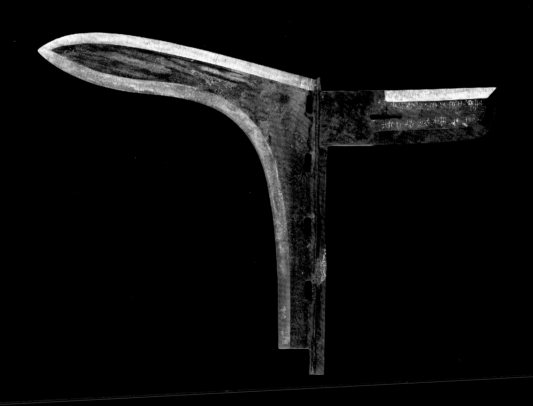

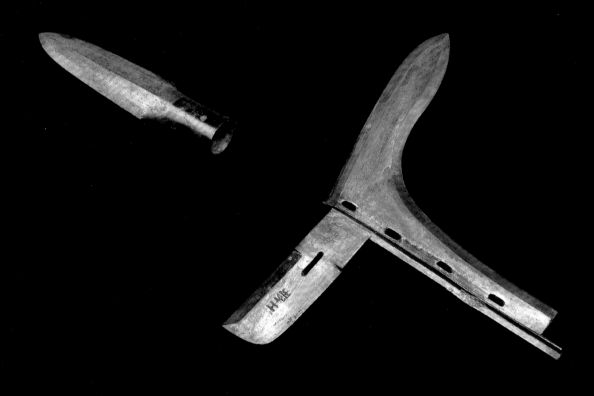

Ji (Halberd)

This is a long-shaft spear with a spear attached to the wooden handle and a dagger-axe on one side. It can also be used for hooking and piercing. Four of them have been unearthed from Pit No.1. This one was broken when it was unearthed. The inscription on it indicates the time of making and the name of the craftsman (it was made by craftsman Jing supervised by officer Zhou under prime minister Lv Buwei).

Pi (A Double-blade Spear with Long Shaft)

Sixteen *pi* have been excavated from terracotta warriors pits. This one 35.3*cm* in length was from Pit No.1, with the time of being made and the name of craftsman engraved on the surface. Its inscription reads "Made by craftsman Diao under Sigong Jiao in the 17th year of the First Emperor". Like a regular spear, *pi* is also a long-shaft weapon. However, it is more powerful because its head acts like a short sword but even sharper and longer.

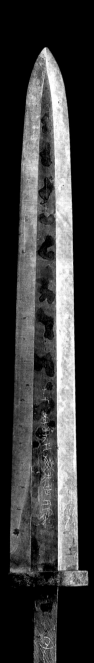

Shu (Club)

Thirty one *shu* have been unearthed from Pit No.1 and No.3, measuring 10.5 ~ 10.6*cm* long and with a diameter of 2.3 ~ 3*cm*. It is a weapon with edge but no blades so it cannot be used for piercing but only for blowing like a mallet. In contrast with spear, halberd and *ge* (dagger-axes), *shu* cannot serve as an effective killing weapon. Therefore, back to the Spring and Autumn period, *shu* was often employed as a ritual weapon instead of a weapon for real battle.

Dun (Spear Shaft End)

There are three types of bronze *dun* unearthed which are all installed on the rear part of a shaft weapon for protection of the handle.

Ji (Halberd) Unearthed from Pit No.1 and the Remains of Its Bi (Shaft)

All the long-shaft weapons unearthed were installed on *bi* (shaft) made of wood or bamboo which has already decayed when excavated. Judging from the 32 traces of remains, *bi* is usually 300 ~ 345*cm* long, painted with brown lacquer and decorated vermilion stripes.

Crossbow

It is a long-range shooting weapon. One hundred and fifty eight crossbows have been found in Pit No.1. This crossbow consists of *xuandao* (trigger), *wangshan* (peep hole) and *gouya* (hook), measuring 16*cm* in length with its *xuandao* in a specification of 10.2*2*0.9*cm*.

Arrowheads

These are the small-sized arrowheads measuring 16.5 ~ 20*cm* long in a perfect triangle shape. The three arched surfaces meet on one end to form a sharp point; on the other end is a flat with three little pricks. The arrowhead looks like a semi-auto riffle bullet excelled with its excellent trajectory, powerful piercing ability and easy manufacturing. All these arrowheads are almost in the same size which reflects the standardized weapon manufacture in Qin dynasty.

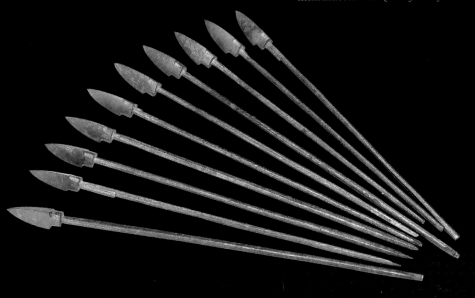

The 3rd Excavation in Pit No.1

After being certified as a leading archaeological team, the Emperor Qin Shi Huang's Mausoleum Site Museum began to carry out the 3rd large archaeological excavation in Pit No.1 on June 13th 2009. The excavation site was in T23 trial pit in the middle of the northern side of the pit, covering a total area of 400m^2. By the end of 2012, two chariots, three sets of 12 terracotta horses, around 170 terracotta figures and nearly 400 pieces (sets) of small objects have been unearthed. Around 10 important relics including military drums, *qie* (suitcase), *bi* (weapon shaft), crossbows, and crossbow quivers have been discovered.

Terracotta Figures of Charioteers

The Charioteer Unearthed in the
3rd Excavation in Pit No.1

Terracotta Figures of High-ranking Officers

A High-ranking Officer Unearthed in the 3rd Excavation in Pit No.1

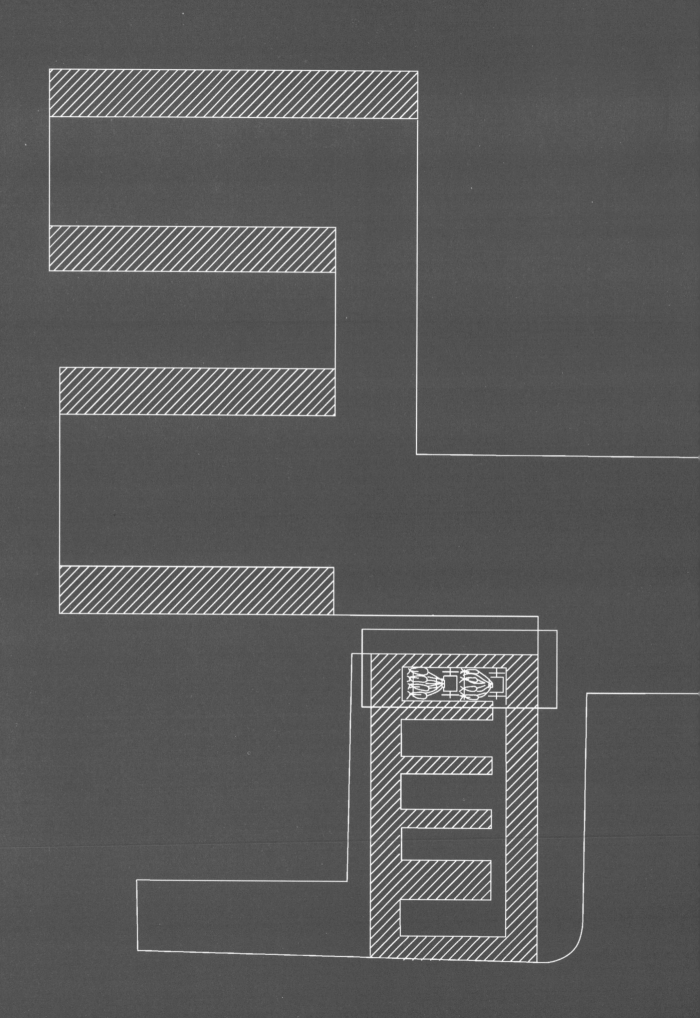

Bronze Chariot Pit

Archeologists excavated two painted bronze chariots in large scale $20m$ west of the mausoleum mound, $7.8m$ underground. As burial objects, the bronze chariots represent Emperor Qin Shi Huang's vehicles.

Each bronze chariot has a single shaft, double wheels and four horses. The two horses in the middle were called *fu* horses used for carrying shaft. The other two, known as *can* horses on the side were facilitating *fu* horses in pulling the chariot. This set of bronze chariots is numbered in accordance with excavation sequence.

Crowned as "the King of the Bronze Ware", the bronze chariots are the earliest, largest, best-preserved bronze artifacts in the world. They revealed Qin dynasty's chariot driving technique, superb bronze-casting technique and magnificent color painting art, serving as a great asset to study Chinese chariot system, bronze-casting techniques and mining techniques.

Bronze Chariot No.1 (Gaoche)

Chariot No.1, also known as *liche* (standing chariot) or *gaoche* (high chariot), measures 225*cm* long, 152*cm* high and weights 1,061*kg*. Drawn by four bronze horses, the chariot has a rectangular cart open on all four sides. Inside the cart stands a copper umbrella with a high rod. Under the umbrella is a standing charioteer. The vehicle is also equipped with a bronze crossbow, a bronze shield, and bronze arrowheads. The chariot is supposed to be a leading military chariot in the imperial cavalcade.

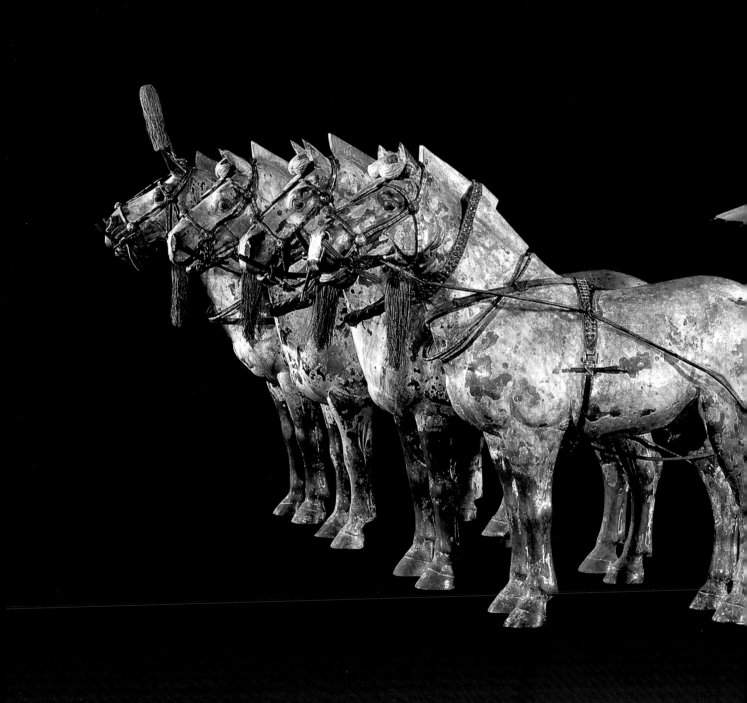

Bronze Chariot No.2 (Anche)

Also known as *anche* (comfort chariot), Chariot No.2 is 317*cm* long, 106.2*cm* high and weights 1,241*kg*. In a convex shape from the plan view, the cart is divided into the front chamber in which sits a charioteer, and the back one in which sits the master. The cart can be opened from three sides even in nowadays. Inside the cart there are serviette and a square jar for the master.

Bronze Shield

As the protection equipment in Chariot No.1, the bronze shield is 36.2*cm* high, 23.5*cm* wide at the bottom edge and measures 0.4*cm* thick. In the center of the front is a stripe of bump with symmetrical ornament on each side; on the axle of the back is a handle. The shield is painted with rich and graceful floating cloud motif and stylized dragons which are well-preserved till nowadays.

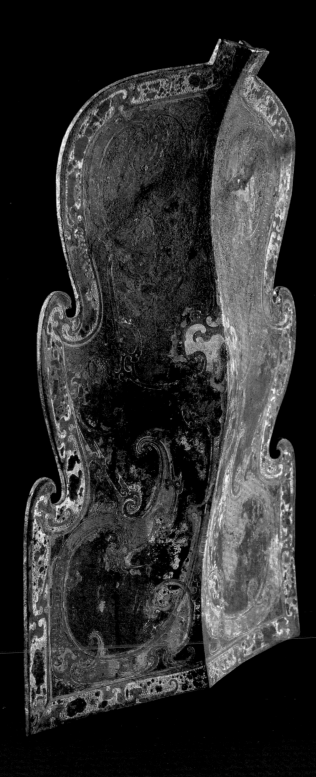

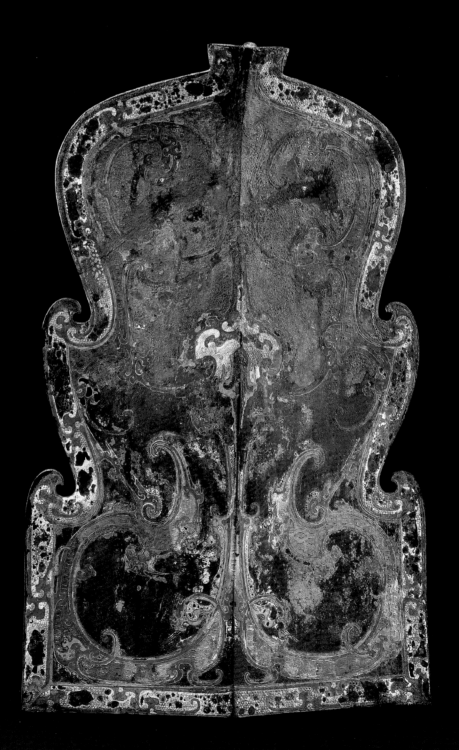

It is one of the components of the umbrella rod in Chariot No.1. The umbrella rod looks like bamboo joints due to the string patterns located on the up, middle and bottom of the rod. The string pattern divides the rod into four sections, each inlaid with gold and silver dragons and phoenixes.

Canopy Handle Inlaid with Gold and Silver Patterns

Gold Danglu (Ornament for Horse Face)

This is one of the gold components of the bronze chariot, fixed on the center of a horse's forehead. It is divided into two layers: the front layer is gold and the back layer is copper plate in the same shape with 4 holes connecting the chains from four directions together not only for decoration but also for speed control.

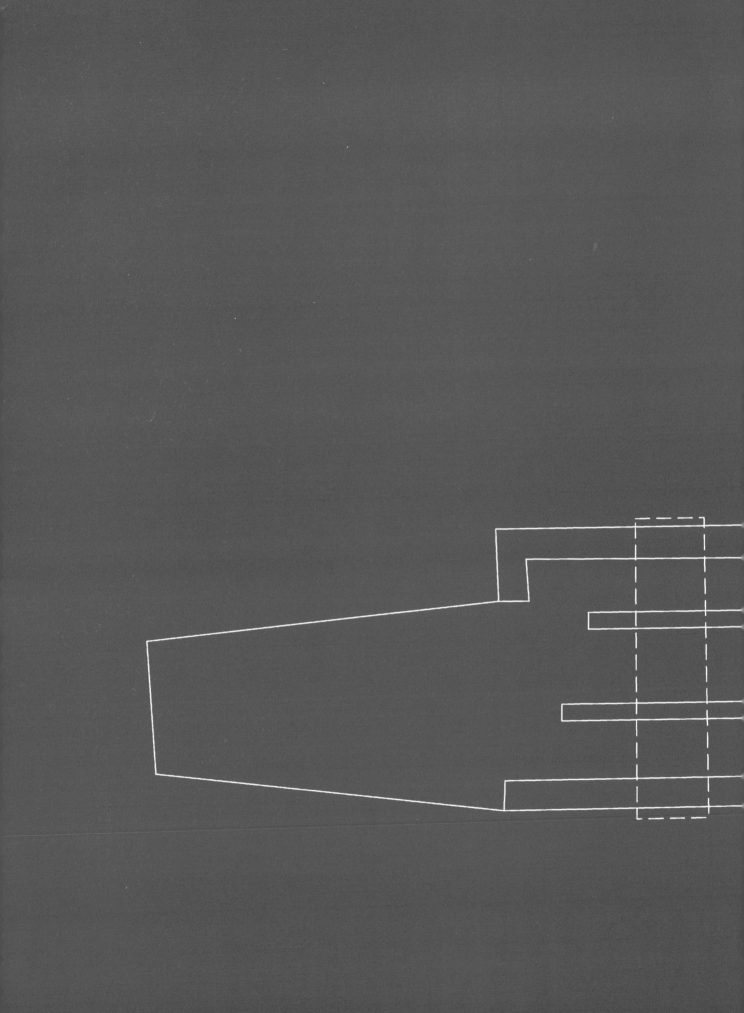

Sacrificial Pit K9901

Pit K9901 was found southeast to Qin Shi Huang's tomb mound, between the inner and the outer walls. It is in convex shape in plan view, covering a total area of $700m^2$. It used to be a $5m$ deep underground tunnel made of a mixture of earth and wood, but collapsed after a fire. One bronze vessel and 11 terracotta figures were unearthed in trial excavation.

In different positions, the 11 life-sized terracotta figures wear no tops but colorful skirts, believed to be a new type of terracotta figure seen for the first time in archeological studies regarding Emperor Qin Shi Huang's mausoleum. According to the documentary, they are believed to be acrobats performing for the imperial court. Therefore, the pit is tentatively names as *Acrobat Pit*.

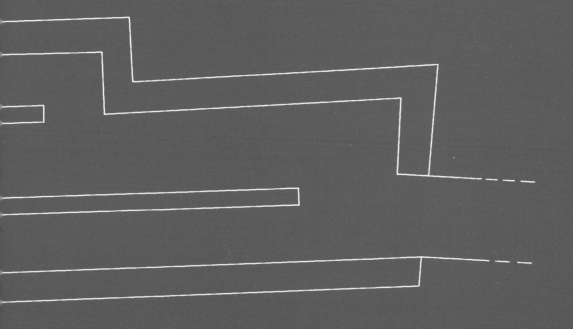

Bai Xi, was the general name for acrobatics in ancient times, including *kangding* (raise a bronze vessel over shoulder), *xuntong* (pole-climbing), *jueli* (wrestling), *paiyou* (comedian), etc. Judging from the gestures of figures unearthed in trial excavation, they are performing *kangding*, *xuntong* and *xuanpan* (disc spinning). It is believed that more figures in various gestures performing acrobatic programs will be discovered in the future as the excavation progresses.

Acrobat No.1

Found without head, remain of this figure is only 152*cm* tall. It has three Chinese characters inscribed on the right arm, indicating the name and hometown of the craftsman who made it. The figure is in a static and peaceful posture, which is quite effective in leaving room for imagination.

Acrobat No.2

This figure is 180*cm* tall with his right hand pointing upwards and left leg bending backwards, in a position as a pheasant standing on one foot. Although we cannot tell which acrobatic program he is performing, its precise body proportion and balance make it shine out as one of the top-rank artifacts among all terracotta figures and sculptures.

Acrobat No.3

Found with no head, remain of this figure is 172*cm* tall. The bare-chested figure looks muscular and in a good shape. It is believed to be a man of unusual strength judging from his posture.

Acrobat No.4

The head-less remain of this figure is 152*cm* tall, posing as if he was lifting a heavy object.

Acrobat No.6

The head-less remains of this figure is 181*cm* in height. He looks very strong and is lifting a heavy object different from that of Acrobat No.4.

Acrobat No.11

The head-less remains of this figure is 152*cm* in height. It has unusual strength judging from its muscular body.

Excavation in sacrificial Pit K9901 has been in full swing since June 2011. By the end of 2012, 28 terracotta figures and one sphere-shape bronze ware have been unearthed after cleaning up corridor No.3. This excavation has deepened the understanding of the nature of this pit; and for the first time fully dressed figures (*paoding terracotta figures*) were discovered in this pit. Currently, repair work goes side by side with ongoing excavation.

Acrobat Figure No.3 (2012)

Unearthed in the eastern side of corridor No.3, it lied on its stomach against the floor when excavated. The upper and the lower body were separated and its head was missing.

Acrobat Figure No.4 (2012)

Unearthed from west side of corridor No.3, the remains of this figure is 157 cm high, lying on the stomach against the floor when unearthed. Its head, both arms and torso were separated. The figure is barefooted dressed in top decorated with round bubbles and skirt with stylized cloud and dragon motif.

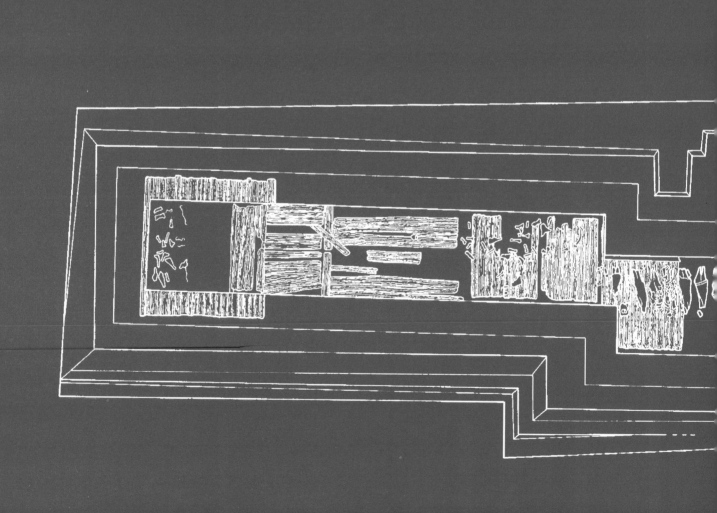

Sacrificial Pit K0006

Located southeast to Qin Shi Huang's tomb mound inside the inner wall, sacrificial Pit K0006 is a *zhong*-shaped (中) earth-wood structure covering a total area of $410m^2$, consisting of a sloping corridor, a front chamber and a back chamber. Its wooden structure remains intact, as it has never suffered from fire.

The front and the back chamber are two independent ones with different objects inside. The front chamber contains 12 terracotta figures, including eight *xiushou* Figures (figures with hands inside their sleeves) and four charioteers. All of them however were broken when unearthed. The degree of damage and wreckages suggest deliberate sabotage shortly after the completion of the pit and even before the woodshed collapsed. Since October 2011, archeology research team No.2 of Emperor Qin Shi Huang's Mausoleum began to clean the back chamber and found 16 sets of identifiable horse bones, lined up with their heads facing north and hips south. Based on the density of the arrangement, it is estimated that more than 20 real horses were buried inside. Scholars have divided opinions on the functionality of this pit, such as for civil officers, for barn, for preparation of horses and chariots before expedition. Currently, the excavation of the pit has finished yet the discussion of its purpose continues.

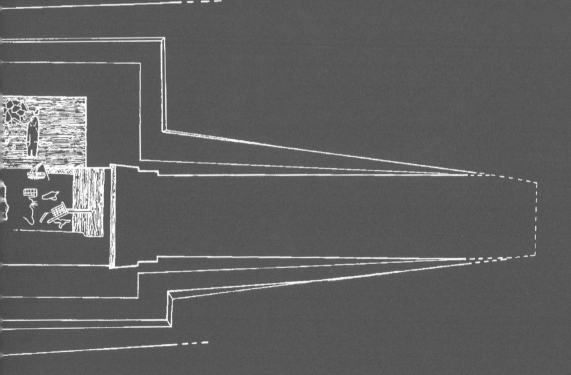

Xiushou Figure No.9 (Figure with Hands inside Sleeves)

This figure is 184*cm* tall with a shoulder width of 44*cm*. It has a knife and stone sharpener hanging from its belt on the right side. An oval hole is both in the left arm and in its torso but no objects are found inside.

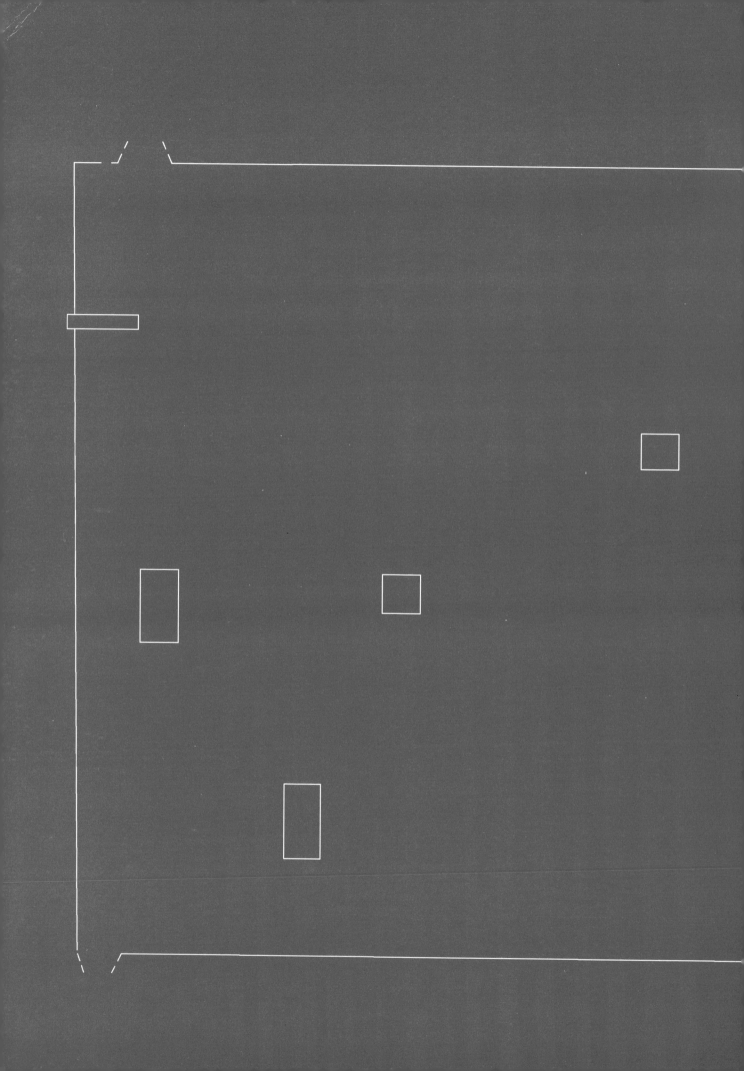

Sacrificial Pit K9801

Sacrificial Pit K9801 situates between the inner and the outer walls $200m$ to the southeast of the tomb mound. In a rectangular shape with a total area of more than $13,000m^2$, the pit is the biggest one found within the wall of the mausoleum. Enormous number of stone armors and stone helmets were unearthed in an area of $145m^2$ through trial excavation. The relatively intact 87 sets of stone armors and 43 stone helmets are useful sources for studying the armory and equipment in Qin dynasty.

Armor without Pauldrons

This 64*cm* long armor without pauldrons, consisting of a front piece and a back piece made up of 380 plates in total. It can be opened through the joint between the chest and the right shoulder. This kind of armor was designed to protect chest, abdomen, back, both sides of the upper body, hips and shoulder tips.

Armor with Pauldrons

Measuring 75cm long, with 20cm long pauldrons, the armor consists of front and back pieces made up of 612 plates, which provide extra protection for shoulders. By using more plates in smaller size, this kind of armor was crafted more exquisitely.

Zhou, the helmet of ancient warriors, is also known as *doumou*. According the historic documents, Qin armies were equipped with helmets as early as the Spring and Autumn period. In ancient times, helmets could be made of copper, leather or iron. In Western Han dynasty, iron gradually took place of leather, becoming the primary helmet material. The stone helmets unearthed in Emperor Qin Shi Huang's mausoleum were the first discovery of this kind. The bluestone helmets however are replica of real helmets and cannot provide protection. So they only serve as burial objects.

Judging from the shapes and assembly methods of helmet plates, there are two dominant types of stone helmets; the first type accounts for more than 90% of the total, and the second type takes a proportion of 3%.

The discovery of Qin helmet artifacts has provided the first sample for study. The stone helmet pieced together with copper wires and stone plates was incomparable in both China and world's archeological history.

Stone Helmet

The stone helmet is 31.5*cm* high, 31.5*cm* wide at the bottom and weights 3,168*g*. It is weaved together with 74 stone plates and copper wires. Coping after leather helmet, its top piece is in semi-sphere shape made of curved plates.

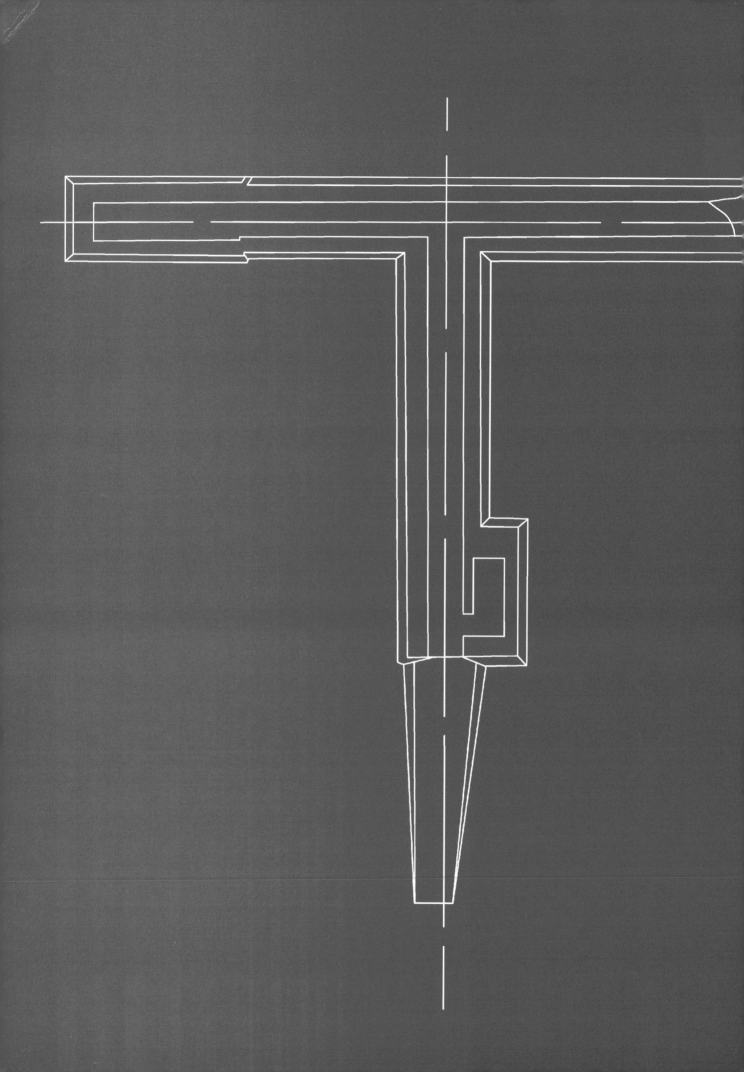

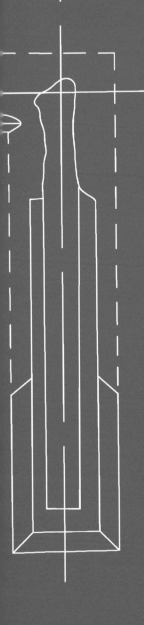

Sacrificial Pit K0007

F-shaped in plan view, this $978m^2$ pit is located $900m$ north to the northeast corner of the tomb mound. Precious cultural relics like bronze aquatic birds and life-size terracotta figures were excavated from this pit, making it a new type of sacrificial pit in the entire mausoleum.

The bronze aquatic birds are categorized into three kinds, bronze swans, bronze cranes and bronze geese, totaling 46 pieces. They are either in standing or lying position, with traces of white paint of different degrees.

Fifteen life-size terracotta figures have been unearthed, including seven terracotta kneeling figures and eight terracotta *Zuozhou* (Rowing) figures. Both groups are dressed in the same costume and look like carrying out some indoor activity or playing on a long couch.

Bronze Wild Goose

In total, 20 pieces of bronze wild geese were excavated in Pit K0007. This piece of bronze swan is 40*cm* tall and 48*cm* long, with its neck and head lifted high as if it was carefully listening.

Bronze Swan

Twenty bronze swans have been unearthed in Pit K0007. This piece of bronze swan is 39.5*cm* high, 91.5*cm* long, bending long neck, tucking its wings as if it was lying down for a nap.

Bronze Crane

Six bronze cranes were discovered in this pit. This one measures 77.5*cm* in height, 112*cm* in length and 18*cm* in width. With its head facing downward, it holds a wriggling worm in its long beak. The sculpture vividly captures the moment when the crane was catching food.

Kneeling Terracotta Figure

Keeping its upper body upright, the kneeling terracotta figure wears only cloth socks with the top of its toes against the ground. He lifts his right arm with the elbow slightly bent and an instrument with sharp corners in hand. Some scholars suggest that he is playing a musical instrument such as a bell or a drum.

Terracotta Figure of Zuozhou (Rowing)

With his legs lying flat on the floor and arms outstretched resting on the knees, the terracotta rowing figure slightly leans his upper body forward. His left hand is half closed with the palm upwards and the other is half closed with the palm downwards as if he was holding an object. It is therefore named as figure of *zuozhou* (rowing) according to its gesture.

图书在版编目(CIP)数据

秦始皇帝陵珍宝 ： 英文 / 秦始皇帝陵博物院编.
—西安 ： 陕西旅游出版社，2013.8
　　ISBN 978-7-5418-2936-9

　Ⅰ．①秦… Ⅱ．①秦… Ⅲ．①秦始皇陵—考古发掘—
图集 Ⅳ．①K878.82

中国版本图书馆CIP数据核字（2013）第196994号

秦始皇帝陵珍宝（英文版）　　　　　　　　　　　秦始皇帝陵博物院 编

责任编辑：王伟 赵璇
出版发行：陕西旅游出版社（西安市唐兴路6号　邮编：710075）
电　　话：029-85252285
经　　销：全国新华书店
印　　刷：深圳市精彩印联合印务有限公司

开　　本：889mm×1194mm　　　1/16
印　　张：10
版　　次：2013年8月　第1版
印　　次：2013年8月　第1次印刷
书　　号：ISBN 978-7-5418-2936-9

定　　价：150.00元